Christopher Gist

Instructions Given Mr. Christopher Gist

By the Committee of the Ohio Company the 11th day of September 1750

Christopher Gist

Instructions Given Mr. Christopher Gist
By the Committee of the Ohio Company the 11th day of September 1750

ISBN/EAN: 9783337251482

Printed in Europe, USA, Canada, Australia, Japan

Cover: Foto ©ninafisch / pixelio.de

More available books at **www.hansebooks.com**

INSTRUCTIONS given Mr CHRISTOPHER GIST by the Comittee of the Ohio Company the 11th Day of September 1750.

YOU are to go out as soon as possible to the Westward of the great Mountains, and carry with you such a Number of Men, as You think necessary, in Order to search out and discover the Lands upon the River Ohio, & other adjoining Branches of the Missisippi down as low as the great Falls thereof : You are particularly to observe the Ways & Passes thro all the Mountains you cross, & take an exact Account of the Soil, Quality, & Product of the Land, and the Wideness & Deepness of the Rivers, & the several Falls belonging to them, together with the Courses & Bearings of the Rivers & Mountains as near as you conveniently can : You are also to observe what Nations of Indians inhabit there, their Strength & Numbers, who they trade with, & in what Comodities they deal.

When you find a large Quantity of good, level Land, such as you think will suit the Company, You are to measure the Breadth of it, in three or four different Places, & take the Courses of the River and Mountains on which it binds in Order to judge the Quantity : You are to fix the Beginning & Bounds in such a Manner that they may be easily found again by your Description ; the nearer in the Land lies, the better, provided it be good & level, but we had rather go quite down the Missisippi than take mean broken Land. After finding a large Body of good level Land, you are not to stop, but proceed farther, as low as the Falls of the Ohio, that We may be informed of that Navigation ; And You are to take an exact Account of all the large Bodies of good level Land, in the same Manner as above directed, that the Company may the better judge where it will be most convenient for them to take their Land.

You are to note all the Bodies of good Land as you go along, tho there is not a sufficient Quantity for the Company's Grant, but You need not be so particular in the Mensuration of that, as in the larger Bodies of Land.

You are to draw as good a Plan as you can of the Country You pass thro : You are to take an exact and particular Journal of all your Proceedings, and make a true Report thereof to the Ohio Company.

1750.

N Complyance with my Instructions from the Committee of the Ohio Company bearing Date the 11th Day of September 1750

Wednesday Octr 31
Set out from Col^o Thomas Cresap's at the old Town on Potomack River in Maryland, and went along an old Indian Path N 30 E about 11 Miles.

Thursday Novr 1
Then N 1 Mile N 30 E 3 M here I was taken sick and stayed all Night.

Friday 2
N 30 E 6 M, here I was so bad that I was not able to proceed any farther that Night, but grew better in the Morning.

Saturday 3
N 8 M to Juniatta, a large Branch of Susquehannah, where I stayed all Night.

Sunday 4
Crofsed Juniatta and went up it S 55 W about 16 M.

Monday 5
Continued the same Course S 55 W 6 M to the Top of a large Mountain called the Allegany Mountain, here our Path turned, & we went N 45 W 6 M here we encamped.

Tuesday 6 Wednesday 7 and Thursday 8
Had Snow and such bad Weather that We could not travel for three Days: but I killed a young Bear so that we had Provision enough.

Friday 9
Set out N 70 W about 8 M here I crofsed a Creek of Susquehannah and it raining hard, I went into an old Indian Cabbin where I stay'd all Night.

Saturday 10
Rain and Snow all Day but cleared away in the Evening

Sunday 11
Set out late in the Morning N 70 W 6 M crofsing two Forks of a Creek of Susquehannah, here the Way being bad, We encamped and I killed a Turkey.

Monday 12
Set out N 45 W 8 M crofsed a great Laurel Mountain.

Tuesday 13
Rain and Snow.

Wednesday 14
Set out N 45 W 6 M to Loylhannan an old Indian Town on a Creek of Ohio called Kiscominatis, then N 1 M NW 1 M to an Indian's Camp on the said Creek.

Thursday 15
The Weather being bad and I unwell I stayed here all Day: The Indian to whom this Camp belonged spoke good English and directed Me the Way to his Town, which is called Shannopini Town: He said it was about 60 M and a pretty good Way.

Friday 16
Set out S 70 W 10 M.

Saturday 17
The same Course (S 70 W) 15 M to an old Indian's Camp

Sunday 18
I was very sick, and sweated myself according to the Indian Custom in a Sweat-House, which gave Me Ease, and my Fever abated.

Monday 19
Set out early in the Morning the same Course (S 70 W) travelled very hard about 20 M to a small Indian Town of the Delawares called Shannopin on the SE Side of

the River Ohio, where We rested and got Corn for our Horses.

Tuesday 20 Wednesday 21 Thursday 22 and Friday 23

I was unwell and stayed in this Town to recover myself; While I was here I took an Opportunity to set my Compaſs privately, & took the Distance acroſs the River, for I understood it was dangerous to let a Compaſs be seen among these Indians: The River Ohio is 76 Poles wide at Shannopin Town: There are about twenty Families in this Town: The Land in general from Potomack to this Place is mean stony and broken, here and there good Spots upon the Creeks and Branches but no Body of it.

Saturday 24

Set out from Shannopin's Town, and swam our Horses acroſs the River Ohio, & went down the River S 75 W 4 M, N 75 W 7 M W 2 M, all the Land from Shannopin's Town is good along the River, but the Bottoms not broad; At a Distance from the River good Land for Farming, covered with small white and red Oaks and tolerable level; fine Runs for Mills &c.

Sunday Novʳ 25

Down the River W 3 M, NW 5 M to the Logg's Town; the Lands these last 8 M very rich the Bottoms above a Mile wide, but on the SE side, scarce a Mile wide, the Hills high and steep. In the Loggs Town, I found scarce any Body but a Parcel of reprobate Indian Traders, the Chiefs of the Indians being out a hunting: here I was informed that George Croghan & Andrew Montour who were sent upon an Embaſsy from Pensylvania to the Indians, were paſsed about a Week before me. The People in this Town, began to enquire my Busineſs, and because I did not readily inform them, they began to suspect me, and said, I was come to settle the Indian's Lands and they knew I should never go Home again safe; I found this Dis-

course was like to be of ill Consequence to me, so I pretended to speak very slightingly of what they had said to me. and enquired for Croghan (who is a meer Idol among his Countrymen the Irish Traders) and Andrew Montour the Interpreter for Pensylvania, and told them I had a Meſsage to deliver the Indians from the King, by Order of the President of Virginia, & for that Reason wanted to see Mʳ Montour: This made them all pretty easy (being afraid to interrupt the King's Meſsage) and obtained me Quiet and Respect among them, otherwise I doubt not they woud have contrived some Evil against me—I iṁediately wrote to Mʳ Croghan, by one of the Trader's People.

Monday 26

Tho I was unwell, I prefered the Woods to such Company & set out from the Loggs Town down the River NW 6 M to great Beaver Creek where I met one Barny Curran a Trader for the Ohio Company, and We continued together as far as Moskingum. The Bottoms upon the River below the Logg's Town very rich but narrow, the high Land pretty good but not very rich, the Land upon Beaver Creek the same kind; From this Place We left the River Ohio to the SE & travelled acroſs the Country

Tuesday 27

Set out from the E side of Beaver Creek NW 6 M, W 4 M; up these two last Courses very good high Land, not very broken, fit for farming.

Wednesday 28

Rained, We could not travel.

Thursday 29

W 6 M thro good Land, the same Course continued 6 M farther thro very broken Land; here I found myself pretty well recovered, & being in Want of Provision, I went out and killed a Deer.

Friday 30

Set out S 45 W 12 M crofsed the last Branch of Beaver Creek where one of Curran's Men & myself killed 12 Turkeys.

Saturdy Decr 1

N 45 W 10 M the Land high and tolerable good.

NOTE by Mr Gist's Plat he makes these 2 Courses N 45 W 10 M, & N 45 W 8 M, to be W 8 M and N 45 W 6 M.

Sunday 2

N 45 W 8 M the same Sort of Land, but near the Crecks bushy and very full of Thorns.

Monday 3

Killed a Deer, and stayed in our Camp all Day.

Tuesday 4

Set out late S 45 W about 4 M here I killed three fine fat Deer, so that tho we were eleven in Company, We had great Plenty of Provision.

Wednesday 5

Set out down the Side of a Creek called Elk's Eye Creek S 70 W 6 M, good Land, but void of Timber, Meadows upon the Creek, fine Runs for Mills.

Thursday 6

Rained all Day so that we were obliged to continue in our Camp.

Friday 7

Set out SW 8 M crofsing the said Elk's Eye Creek to a Town of the Ottaways, a Nation of French Indians ; an old French Man (named Mark Coonce) who had married an Indian Woman of the six Nations iived here ; the Indians were all out a hunting ; the old Man was very civil to me, but after I was gone to my Camp, upon his understanding I came from Virginia, he called Me the Big Knife. There are not above six or eight Families belonging to this Town.

Saturday 8

Stayed in the Town.

Sunday 9

Set out down the said Elk's Eye Creek S 45 W 6 M to Margarets Creek a Branch of the said Elk's Eye Creek.

Monday Decr 10

The same Course (S 45 W) 2 M to a large Creek.

Tuesday 11

The same Course 12 M killed 2 Deer.

Wednesday 12

The same Course 8 M encamped by the Side of Elk's Eye Creek

Thursday 13

Rained all Day.

Friday 14

Set out W 5 M to Moskingum a Town of the Wyendotts. The Land upon Elk's Eye Creek is in general very broken, the Bottoms narrow. The Wyendotts or little Mingoes are divided between the French and English, one half of them adhere to the first, and the other half are firmly attached to the latter. The Town of Moskingum consists of about one hundred Families. When We came within Sight of the Town, We percieved English Colours hoisted on the King's House, and at George Croghan's ; upon enquiring the Reason I was informed that the French had lately taken several English Traders, and that Mr Croghan had ordered all the White Men to come into this Town, and had sent Exprefses to the Traders of the lower Towns, and among the Pickweylinees ; and the Indians had sent to their People to come to Council about it.

Saturday 15 & Sunday 16

Nothing remarkable happened.

Monday 17

Came into Town two Traders belonging to Mr Croghan, and informed Us that two of his People were taken by 40 French Men, & twenty French Indians who had carried them with seven Horse Loads of Skins to a new Fort that the French were building on one of the Branches of Lake Erie

Tuesday 18

I acquainted Mr Croghan and Andrew Montour with my Busineſs with the Indians, & talked much of a Regulation of Trade with which they were much pleased, and treated Me very kindly.

From Wednesday 19 to Monday 24 Nothing remarkable.

Tuesday 25

This being Christmaſs Day, I intended to read Prayers, but after inviting some of the White Men, they informed each other of my Intentions, and being of several different Persuasions, and few of them inclined to hear any Good, they refused to come. But one Thomas Burney a Black Smith who is settled there went about and talked to them, & then several of them came ; and Andrew Montour invited several of the well disposed Indians, who came freely ; by this Time the Morning was spent, and I had given over all Thoughts of them, but seeing Them come, to oblige All, and offend None, I stood up and said, Gentlemen, I have no Design or Intention to give Offence to any particular Sectary or Religion, but as our King indulges Us all in a Liberty of Conscience and hinders none of You in the Exercise of your religious Worship, so it woud be unjust in You, to endeavour to stop the Propagation of His ; The Doctrine of Salvation Faith, and good Works, is what I only propose to treat of, as I find it extracted from the Homilies of the Church of England, which I then read to them in the best Manner I coud, and after I had done the Interpreter

told the Indians what I had read, and that it was the true Faith which the great King and his Church recomended to his Children : the Indians seemed well pleased, and came up to Me and returned Me their Thanks ; and then invited Me to live among Them, and gave Me a Name in their Language Annosanah : the Interpreter told Me this was a Name of a good Man that had formerly lived among them, and their King said that must be always my Name, for which I returned them Thanks ; but as to living among them I excused myself by saying I did not know whether the Governor woud give Me Leave, and if he did the French woud come and carry me away as they had done the English Traders, to which they answered I might bring great Guns and make a Fort, that they had now left the French, and were very desirous of being instructed in the Principles of Christianity ; that they liked Me very well and wanted Me to marry Them after the Christian Manner, and baptize their Children ; and then they said they woud never desire to return to the French, or suffer Them or their Priests to come near them more, for they loved the English, but had seen little Religion among Them : and some of their great Men came and wanted Me to baptize their Children ; for as I had read to Them and appeared to talk about Religion they took Me to be a Minister of the Gospel : Upon which I desired Mr Montour (the Interpreter) to tell Them, that no Minister coud venture to baptize any Children, until those that were to be Sureties for Them, were well instructed in the Faith themselves, and that this was according to the great King's Religion, in which He desired his Children shoud be instructed, & We dare not do it in any other Way, than was by Law established, but I hoped if I coud not be admitted to live among them, that the great King woud send Them proper Ministers to exercise that Office among them, at which they seemed well pleased ; and one of Them went and brought Me his Book (which was a Kind contrived for Them by the French in which the Days of the Week were so marked that by moving a Pin every Morning they kept a pretty exact Account of the Time) to shew Me that he understood Me, and that He and his Family always observed the Sabbath Day.

Wednesday Dec.ʳ 26

This Day a Woman, who had been a long Time a Prisoner, and had deserted, & been retaken, and brought into the Town on Christmafs Eve, was put to Death in the following Manner: They carried Her without the Town, & let her loose, and when she attempted to run away, the Persons appointed for that Purpose pursued her, & struck Her on the Ear, on the right Side of her Head, which beat her flat on her Face on the Ground; they then stuck her several Times, thro the Back with a Dart, to the Heart, scalped Her, & threw the Scalp in the Air, and another cut off her Head: There the dismal Spectacle lay till the Evening, & then Barny Curran desired Leave to bury Her, which He, and his Men, and some of the Indians did just at Dark.

From Thursday Dec.ʳ 27 to Thursday Jan.ʸ 3 1751

Nothing remarkable happened in the Town.

Friday Jan.ʸ 4

One Teafe (an Indian Trader) came to Town from near Lake Erie, & informed Us, that the Wyendott Indians had advised Him to keep clear of the Ottaways (these are a Nation of Indians firmly attached to the French, & inhabit near the Lakes) & told Him that the Branches of the Lakes are claimed by the French; but that all the Branches of Ohio belonged to Them, and their Brothers the English, and that the French had no Business there, & that it was expected that the other Part of the Wyendott Nation woud desert the French

and come over to the English Interest, & join their Brethren on the Elk's Eye Creek, & build a strong Fort and Town there.

From Saturday 5 to Tuesday 8

The Weather still continuing bad, I stayed in the Town to recruit my Horses, and tho Corn was very dear among the Indians, I was obliged to feed them well, or run the Risque of losing them as I had a great Way to travel.

Wednesday 9

The Wind Southerly, and the Weather something warmer: this Day came into Town two Traders from among the Pickwaylinees (these are a Tribe of the Twigtwees) and brought News that another English Trader was taken Prisoner by the French, and that three French Soldiers had deserted and come over to the English, and surrendered themselves to some of the Traders of the Pick Town, & that the Indians woud have put them to Death, to revenge their taking our Traders, but as the French Prisoners had surrendered themselves, the English woud not let the Indians hurt them, but had ordered them to be sent under the Care of three of our Traders and delivered at this Town, to George Croghan.

Thursday 10

Wind still at South and warm.

Friday 11

This Day came into Town an Indian from over the Lakes & confirmed the News we had heard.

Saturday 12

We sent away our People towards the lower Town intending to follow them the next Morning, and this Evening We went into Council in the Wyendott's King's House—The Council had been put off a long Time expecting some of their great Men in, but few of them came, & this

Evening some of the King's Council being a little disordered with Liquor, no Busineſs coud be done, but We were desired to come next Day.

Sunday Janʳʸ 13
No Busineſs done.

Monday 14
This Day George Croghan, by the Assistance of Andrew Montour, acquainted the King and Council of this Nation (by presenting them four Strings of Wampum) that the great King over the Water, their Roggony [Father] had sent under the Care of the Governor of Virginia, their Brother, a large Present of Goods which was now landed safe in Virginia, & the Governor had sent Me to invite Them to come and see Him, & partake of their Father's Charity to all his Children on the Branches of Ohio. In Answer to which one of the Chiefs stood up and said, "That their " King and all of Them thanked their " Brother the Governor of Virginia for his " Care, and Me for bringing them the " News, but they coud not give Me an " Answer untill they had a full or general " Council of the several Nations of Indians " which coud not be till next Spring: & " so the King and Council shaking Hands " with Us, We took our Leave.

Tuesday 15
We left Moskingum, and went W 5 M, to the White Woman's Creek. on which is a small Town; this White Woman was taken away from New England, when she was not above ten Years old, by the French Indians; She is now upwards of fifty, and has an Indian Husband and several Children—Her Name is Mary Harris, she still remembers they used to be very religious in New England, and wonders how the White Men can be so wicked as she has seen them in these Woods.

Wednesday 16
Set out SW 25 M, to Licking Creek—

The Land from Moskingum to this Place rich but broken—Upon the N Side of Licking Creek about 6 M from the Mouth, are several Salt Licks, or Ponds, formed by little Streams or Dreins of Water, clear but of a blueish Colour, & salt Taste, the Traders and Indians boil their Meat in this Water, which (if proper Care be not taken) will sometimes make it too salt to eat.

Thursday 17
Set out W 5 M, SW 15 M, to a great Swamp.

Friday 18
Set out from the great Swamp SW 15 M.

Saturday 19
W 15 M to Hockhockin a small Town with only four or five Delaware Families.

Sunday 20
The Snow began to grow thin, and the Weather warmer; Set out from Hockhockin S 5 M, then W 5 M, then SW 5 M, to the Maguck a little Delaware Town of about ten Families by the N Side of a plain or clear Field about 5 M in Length NE & SW, & 2 M broad, with a small Rising in the Middle, which gives a fine Prospect over the whole Plain, and a large Creek on the N Side of it called Sciodoe Creek. All the Way from Licking Creek to this Place is fine rich level Land, with large Meadows, fine Clover Bottoms, & spacious Plains covered with wild Rye: the Wood chiefly large Walnuts and Hickories, here and there mixed with Poplars Cherry Trees and Sugar Trees.

From Monday 21 to Wednesday 23
Stayed in the Maguck Town.

Thursday 24
Set out from the Maguck Town S about 15 M, thro fine rich level Land to a small Town called Harrickintoms consisting of about five or six Delaware Families, on the SW Sciodoe Creek.

Friday 25

The Creek being very high and full of Ice, We coud not ford it, and were obliged to go down it on the SE Side SE 4 M to the Salt Lick Creek—about 1 M up this Creek on the S Side is a very large Salt Lick, the Streams which run into this Lick are very salt, & tho clear leave a blueish Sediment: The Indians and Traders make Salt for their Horses of this Water, by boiling it ; it has at first a blueish Colour, and somewhat bitter Taste, but upon dissolved in fair Water and boiled a second Time, it becomes tolerable pure Salt.

Saturday 26
Set out S 2 M, SW 14 M

Sunday 27

S 12 M to a small Delaware Town of about twenty Families on the SE Side of Sciodoe Creek—We lodged at the House of an Indian whose Name was Windaughalah, a great Man and Chief of this Town, & much in the English Interest. He entertained Us very kindly, and ordered a Negro Man that belonged to him to feed our Horses well; this Night it snowed, and in the Morning tho the Snow was six or seven Inches deep, the wild Rye appeared very green and flourishing thro it, and our Horses had fine Feeding.

Monday Janʸ 28

We went into Council with the Indians of this Town, and after the Interpreter had informed them of his Instructions from the Governor of Pensylvania, and given them some Cautions in Regard to the French, they returned for Answer as follows. The Speaker with four Strings of Wampum in his Hand stood up, and addressing Himself as to the Governor of Pensylvania, said, " Brothers, We the Delawares return You " our hearty Thanks for the News You " have sent Us, and We assure You, We " will not hear the Voice of any other Na-

" tion for We are to be directed by You " our Brothers the English, & by none " else : We shall be glad to hear what our " Brothers have to say to Us at the Loggs " Town in the Spring, and to assure You " of our hearty Good will & Love to our " Brothers We present You with these " four Strings of Wampum This is the last Town of the Delawares to the Westward—The Delaware Indians by the best Accounts I coud gather consist of about 500 fighting Men all firmly attached to the English Interest, they are not properly a Part of the six Nations, but are scattered about among most of the Indians upon the Ohio, and some of them among the six Nations, from whom they have Leave to hunt upon their Lands.

Tuesday 29

Set out SW 5 M, S 5 M to the Mouth of Sciodoe Creek opposite to the Shannoah Town, here We fired our Guns to alarm the Traders, who soon answered, and came and ferryed Us over to the Town—The Land about the Mouth of Sciodoe Creek is rich but broken fine Bottoms upon the River & Creek—The Shannoah Town is situate upon both Sides the River Ohio, just below the Mouth of Sciodoe Creek, and contains about 300 Men, there are about 40 Houses on the S Side of the River and about 100 on the N Side, with a Kind of State-House of about 90 Feet long, with a light Cover of Bark in wᶜʰ they hold their Councils—The Shanaws are not a Part of the six Nations, but were formerly at Variance with them, tho now reconciled : they are great Friends to the English who once protected them from the Fury of the six Nations, which they gratefully remember.

Wednesday 30

We were conducted into Council, where George Croghan delivered sundry Speeches from the Government of Pensylvania to the Chiefs of this Nation, in which He in-

formed them, "That two Prisoners who
" had been taken by the French, and had
" made their Escape from the French
" Officer at Lake Erie as he was carrying
" them towards Canada brought News
" that the French offered a large Sum of
" Money to any Person who woud bring
" to them the said Croghan and Andrew
" Montour the Interpreter alive, or if dead
" their Scalps ; and that the French also
" threatened these Indians and the Wyen-
" dotts with War in the Spring" the same
Persons farther said " that they had seen
" ten French Canoes loaded with Stores
" for a new Fort they designed on the S
Side Lake Erie. Mr Croghan also informed them of several of our Traders
having been taken, and advised them to
keep their Warriors at Home, until they
coud see what the French intended which
he doubted not woud appear in the Spring
—Then Andrew Montour informed this
Nation as He had done the Wyendotts &
Delawares " That the King of Great Britain
" had sent Them a large Present of Goods,
" in Company with the six Nations, which
" was under the Care of the Governor of
" Virginia, who had sent Me out to invite
" them to come and see Him, & partake
" of their Father's Present next Sumer"
to which We received this Answer—Big
Hannaona their Speaker taking in his
Hand the several Strings of Wampum
which had been given by the English, He
said " These are the Speeches received by
" Us from your great Men : From the
" Beginning of our Friendship, all that
" our Brothers the English have told Us
" has been good and true, for which We
" return our hearty Thanks" Then taking
up four other Strings of Wampum in his
Hand, He said " Brothers I now speak the
" Sentiments of all our People : when first
" our Forefathers did meet the English
" our Brothers, they found what our Bro-
" thers the English told them to be true,
" and so have We—We are but a small
" People, & it is not to Us only that You

23

" speak, but to all Nations—We shall be
" glad to hear what our Brothers will say
" to Us at the Loggs Town in the Spring,
" & We hope that the Friendship now
" subsisting between Us & our Brothers,
" will last as long as the Sun shines, or the
" Moon gives Light—We hope that our
" Children will hear and believe what our
" Brothers say to them, as We have always
" done, and to afsure You of our hearty
" Good-Will towards You our Brothers,
" We present You with these four Strings
" of Wampum " After the Council was
over they had much Talk about sending a
Guard with Us to the Pickwaylinees Towns
(these are a Tribe of Twigtwees) which
was reckoned near 200 Miles, but after
long Consultation (their King being sick)
they came to no Determination about it.

From Thursday Jan 31 To Monday
Feby 11
Stayed in the Shannoah Town, while I
was here the Indians had a very extraordinary Kind of a Festival, at which I was
present and which I have exactly described
at the End of my Journal—As I had particular Instructions from the President of
Virginia to discover the Strength & Numbers of some Indian Nations to the Westward of Ohio who had lately revolted from
the French, and had some Mefsages to
deliver them from Him, I resolved to set
out for the Twigtwee Town.

Tuesday 12
Having left my Boy to take Care of my
Horses in the Shannoah Town, & supplied
myself with a fresh Horse to ride, I set
out with my old Company viz George
Croghan Andrew Montour, Robert Kal-
landar, and a Servant to carry our Provi-
sions &c NW 10 M.

Wednesday 13
The same Course (NW) about 35 M.

Thursday 14
The same Course about 30 M.

24

The same Course 15 M. We met with nine Shannoah Indians coming from one of the Pickwaylinees Towns, where they had been to Council, they told Us there were fifteen more of them behind at the Twigtwee Town, waiting for the Arrival of the Wawaughtanneys, who are a Tribe of the Twigtwees, and were to bring with them a Shannoah Woman and Child to deliver to their Men that were behind: this Woman they informed Us had been taken Prisoner last Fall, by some of the Wawaughtanney Warriors thro a Mistake, which had like to have engaged these Nations in a War.

Saturday 16
Set out the same Course (NW) about 35 M, to the little Miamee River or Creek

Sunday 17
Crossed the little Miamee River, and altering our Course We went SW 25 M, to the big Miamee River, opposite the Twigtwee Town. All the Way from the Shannoah Town to this Place (except the first 20 M which is broken) is fine, rich level Land, well timbered with large Walnut, Ash, Sugar Trees, Cherry Trees &c, it is well watered with a great Number of little Streams or Rivulets, and full of beautiful natural Meadows, covered with wild Rye, blue Grass and Clover, and abounds with Turkeys, Deer, Elks and most Sorts of Game particularly Buffaloes, thirty or forty of which are frequently seen feeding in one Meadow: In short it wants Nothing but Cultivation to make it a most delightfull Country—The Ohio and all the large Branches are said to be full of fine Fish of several Kinds, particularly a Sort of Cat Fish of a prodigious Size; but as I was not there at the proper Season, I had not an opportunity of seeing any of them —The Traders had always reckoned it 200 M, from the Shannoah Town to the Twigtwee Town, but by my Computation

I coud make it no more than 150—The Miamee River being high, We were obliged to make a Raft of old Loggs to transport our Goods and Saddles and swim our Horses over—After firing a few Guns and Pistols, & smoaking in the Warriors Pipe, who came to invite Us to the Town (according to their Custom of inviting and welcoming Strangers and Great Men) We entered the Town with English Colours before Us, and were kindly received by their King, who invited Us into his own House, & set our Colours upon the Top of it—The Firing of Guns held about a Quarter of an Hour, and then all the white Men and Traders that were there, came and welcomed Us to the Twigtwee Town—This Town is situate on the NW Side of the Big Miamee River about 150 M from the Mouth thereof; it consists of about 400 Families, & daily encreasing, it is accounted one of the strongest Indian Towns upon this Part of the Continent—The Twigtwees are a very numerous People consisting of many different Tribes under the same Form of Government. Each Tribe has a particular Chief or King, one of which is chosen indifferently out of any Tribe to rule the whole Nation, and is vested with greater Authorities than any of the others—They are accounted the most powerful People to the Westward of the English Settlements, & much superior to the six Nations with whom they are now in Amity: their Strength and Numbers are not thoroughly known, as they have but lately traded with the English, and indeed have very little Trade among them: they deal in much the same Comodities with the Northern Indians. There are other Nations or Tribes still further to the Westward daily coming in to them, & 'tis thought their Power and Interest reaches to the Westward of the Mississippi, if not acrofs the Continent; they are at present very well affećted to the English, and seem fond of an Alliance with them—they formerly lived on the farther Side of the Obache, and were in the French Interest, who supplied them with with some few Trifles at a most exorbitant Price—they were called by the French Miamees; but they have now revolted from them, and left their former Habitations for the Sake of trading with the English; and notwithstanding all the Artifices the French have used, they have not been able to recall them.

After We had been some Time in the King's House Mr Montour told Him that We wanted to speak with Him and the Chiefs of this Nation this Evening upon which We were invited into the long House, and having taken our Places Mr Montour began as follows—" Brothers the Twig-
" twees as We have been hindered by the
" high Waters and some other Busineſs
" with our Indian Brothers, no Doubt our
" long Stay has caused some Trouble among
" our Brethren here, Therefore We now
" present You with two Strings of Wam-
" pum to remove all the Trouble of your
" Hearts, & clear your Eyes, that You may
" see the Sun shine clear, for We have a
" great Deal to say to You, & We woud
" have You send for one of Your Friends
" that can speak the Mohickon or the
" Mingoe Tongues well, that We may un-
" derstand each other thoroughly, for We
" have a great Deal of Busineſs to do "—
The Mohickons are a small Tribe who most of them speak English, and are also well acquainted with the Language of the Twigtwees, and they with theirs—Mr Montour then proceeded to deliver Them a Meſsage from the Wyendotts and Delawares as follows "Brothers the Twigtwees, this comes
" by our Brothers the English who are
" coming with good News to You: We
" hope You will take Care of Them, and
" all our Brothers the English who are
" trading among You: You made a Road
" for our Brothers the English to come
" and trade among You, but it is now very
" foul, great Loggs are fallen acroſs it, and
" We woud have You be strong like Men,
" and have one Heart with Us, and make

" the Road clear, that our Brothers the
" English may have free Course and Re-
" course between You and Us—In the Sin-
" cerity of our Hearts We send You these
" four Strings of Wampum, to which they gave the usual Yo Ho—Then they said they wanted some Tobacco to smoak with Us, and that tomorrow they woud send for their Interpreter.

Monday Feby 18
We walked about viewed the Fort which wanted some Repairs, & the Trader's Men helped Them to bring Loggs to line the Inside.

Tuesday 19
We gave their Kings and great Men some Clothes, and Paint Shirts, and now they were busy dreſsing and preparing themselves for the Council—The Weather grew warm and the Creeks began to lower very fast.

Wednesday 20
About 12 of the Clock We were informed that some of the foreign Tribes were coming, upon which proper Persons were ordered to meet them and conduct Them into the Town, and then We were invited into the long House; after We had been seated about a Quarter of an Hour four Indians, two from each Tribe (who had been sent before to bring the long Pipe, and to inform that the rest were coming) came in, & informed Us that their Friends had sent these Pipes that We might smoak the Calamut Pipe of Peace with Them and that they intended to do the same with Us.

Thursday Feby 21
We were again invited into the long House where Mr Croghan made them (with the foreign Tribes) a Present to the Value of £100 Pensylvania Money, and delivered all our Speeches to Them, at which they seemed well pleased, and said, that they would take Time and consider well what We had said to Them.

Friday 22

Nothing remarkable happened in the Town.

Saturday 23

In the Afternoon there was an Alarm in the Town which caused a great Confusion and running about among the Indians, upon enquiring into the Reason of this Stir, they told Us that it was occasioned by six Indians that came to war against Them, from the Southward: three of them Cutaways, and three Shanaws (these were some of the Shanaws who had formerly deserted from the other Part of the Nation, and now live to the Southward) Towards Night there was a Report spread in Town that four Indians, and four hundred French, were on their March and just by the Town: But soon after the Meſsenger who brought this News said, there were only four french Indians coming to Council, and that they bid him say so, only to see how the English woud behave themselves; but as they had behaved themselves like Men, He now told the Truth.

Sunday 24

This Morning the four French Indians came into Town and were kindly received by the Town Indians; they marched in under French Colours, and were conducted into the long House, and after they had been in about a Quarter of an Hour, the Council sate, and We were sent for that We might hear what the French had to say to them—The Pyankeshee King (who was at that Time the principal Man, and Comander in Chief of the Twigtwees) said, He woud have the English Colours set up in this Council as well as the French, to which We answered he might do as he thought fit. After We were seated right opposite to the French Embassadors, One of Them said, He had a Present to make Them, so a Place was prepared (as they had before done for our Present) between Them and Us, and then their Speaker

stood up, and layed his Hands upon two small Caggs of Brandy that held about seven Quarts each, and a Roll of Tobacco of about ten Pounds Weight, then taking two Strings of Wampum in his Hand, He said, "What he had to deliver Them was "from their Father (meaning the French "King) and he desired they woud hear "what he was about to say to Them;" then he layed them two Strings of Wampum down upon the Caggs, and taking up four other Strings of black and white Wampum, he said, "that their Father remem-"bring his Children, had sent them two "Caggs of Milk, and some Tobacco, and "that he now had made a clear Road for "them, to come and see Him and his "Officers; and pressed them very much "to come; then he took another String of Wampum in his Hand, and said, "their "Father now woud forget all little Dif-"ferences that had been between Them, "and desired Them not to be of two "Minds, but to let Him know their Minds "freely, for He woud send for Them no "more"—To which the Pyankeshee King replyed, "it was true their Father had sent "for them several Times, and said the "Road was clear, but He understood it "was made foul & bloody, and by Them— "We (said He) have cleared a Road for "our Brothers the English, and your Fa-"thers have made it bad, and have taken "some of our Brothers Prisoners, Which "We look upon as done to Us, and he "turned short about and went out of "Council"—After the French Embaſsador had delivered his Meſsage He went into one of the private Houses, and endeavoured much to prevail on some Indians, and was seen to cry and lament (as he said for the Loſs of that Nation.

Monday Feby 25

This Day We received a Speech from the Wawaughtanneys and Pyankeshees (two Tribes of the Twigtwees) One of the Chiefs of the former spoke "Brothers,

" We have heard what You have said to
" Us by the Interpreter and We see You
" take Pity upon our poor Wives and Chil-
" dren, and have taken Us by the Hand
" into the great Chain of Friendship;
" therefore We present You with these
" two Bundles of Skins to make Shoes for
" your People, and this Pipe to smoak
" in, to afsure You that our Hearts are
" good and true towards You our Brothers;
" and We hope that We shall all continue
" in true Love and Friendship with one
" another, as People with one Head and
" one Heart ought to do; You have pi-
" tyed Us as You always did the rest of
" our Indian Brothers, We hope that Pity
" You have always shewn, will remain as
" long as the Sun gives Light, and on our
" Side you may depend upon sincere and
" true Friendship towards You as long as
" We have Strength "—This Person stood
up and spoke with the Air and Gesture of
an Orator.

Tuesday 26

Tho Twigtwees delivered the following
Answer to the four Indians sent by the
French—The Captain of the Warriors
stood up and taking some Strings of black
and white Wampum in his Hand he spoke
with a fierce Tone and very warlike Air—
" Brothers the Ottaways, You are always
" differing with the French Yourselves,
" and yet You listen to what they say, but
" We will let You know by these four
" Strings of Wampum, that We will not
" hear any Thing they say to Us, nor do
" any Thing they bid Us "—Then the
same Speaker with six Strouds two Match-
Coats, and a String of black Wampum (I
understood the Goods were in Return for
the Milk and Tobacco) and directing his
Speech to the French said, " Fathers, You
" desire that We may speak our Minds
" from our Hearts, which I am going
" to do; You have often desired We
" shoud go Home to You, but I tell
" You it is not our Home, for We have
" made a Road as far as the Sea to the

31

" Sun-rising, and have been taken by the
" Hand by our Brothers the English, and
" the six Nations, and the Delawares
" Shannoahs and Wyendotts, and We as-
" sure You it is the Road We will go; and
" as You threaten Us with War in the
" Spring, We tell You if You are angry
" We are ready to receive You, and resolve
" to die here before We will go to You;
" And that You may know that this our
" Mind, We send You this String of black
" Wampum." After a short Pause the
same Speaker spoke again thus—" Bro-
" thers the Ottaways, You hear what I say,
" tell that to your Fathers the French, for
" that is our Mind, and We speak it from
" our Hearts.

Wednesday 27

This Day they took down their French
Colours, and dismifsed the four French Indians, so they took their Leave of the Town
and set off for the French Fort.

Thursday 28

The Crier of the Town came by the
King's Order and invited Us to the long
House to see the Warriors Feather Dance;
it was performed by three Dancing-Mas-
ters, who were painted all over with vari-
ous Colours, with long Sticks in their Hands,
upon the Ends of which were fastened long
Feathers of Swans, and other Birds, neatly
woven in the Shape of a Fowls Wing: in
this Disguise they performed many antick
Tricks, waving their Sticks and Feathers
about with great Skill to imitate the flying
and fluttering of Birds, keeping exact Time
with their Musick; while they are dancing
some of the Warriors strikes a Post, upon
which the Musick and Dancers cease, and
the Warrior gives an Account of his At-
chievements in War, and when he has
done, throws down some Goods as a Re-
compence to the Performers and Musi-
cians; after which they proceed in their
Dance as before till another Warrior strikes

32

ye Post, and so on as long as the Company think fit

Friday March 1

We received the following Speech from the Twigtwees the Speaker stood up and addreſsing himself as to the Governor of Pensylvania with two Strings of Wampum in his Hand, He said—" Brothers our " Hearts are glad that You have taken No- " tice of Us, and surely Brothers We hope " that You will order a Smith to settle here " to mend our Guns and Hatchets, Your " Kindneſs makes Us so bold to ask this " Request. You told Us our Friendship " should last as long, and be as the greatest " Mountain, We have considered well, and " all our great Kings & Warriors are come " to a Resolution never to give Heed to " what the French say to Us, but always " to hear & believe what You our Brothers " say to Us—Brothers We are obliged to " You for your kind Invitation to receive " a Present at the Loggs Town, but as our " foreign Tribes are not yet come, We " must wait for them, but You may de- " pend We will come as soon as our " Women have planted Corn to hear what " our Brothers will say to Us—Brothers " We present You with this Bundle of " Skins, as We are but poor to be for " Shoes for You on the Road, and We " return You our hearty Thanks for the " Clothes which You have put upon our " Wives and Children "—We then took our Leave of the Kings and Chiefs, and they ordered that a small Party of Indians shoud go with Us as far as Hockhockin; but as I had left my Boy & Horses at the lower Shannoah Town, I was obliged to go by myself or to go sixty or seventy Miles out of my Way, which I did not care to do; so we all came over the Miamee River together this Evening, but Mr Croghan & Mr Montour went over again & lodged in the Town, but I stayed on this Side at one Robert Smith's (a Trader) where We had left our Horses—Before the French

33

Indians had come into Town, We had drawn Articles of Peace and Alliance between the English and the Wawaughtanneys and Pyankeshees; the Indentures were signed sealed and delivered on both Sides, and as I drew them I took a Copy— The Land upon the great Miamee River is very rich level and well timbered, some of the finest Meadows that can be: The Indians and Traders aſsure Me that the Land holds as good and if poſsible better, to the Westward as far as the Obache which is accounted 100 Miles, and quite up to the Head of the Miamee River, which is 60 Miles above the Twigtwee Town, and down the said River quite to the Ohio which is reckoned 150 Miles— The Graſs here grows to a great Height in the clear Fields, of which there are a great Number, & the Bottoms are full of white Clover, wild Rye, and blue Graſs.

Saturday March 2

George Croghan and the rest of our Company came over the River, We got our Horses, & set out about 35 M. to Mad Creek (this is a Place where some English Traders had been taken Prisoners by the French.)

Sunday 3

This Morning We parted, They for Hockhockin, and I for the Shannoah Town, and as I was quite alone and knew that the French Indians had threatened Us, and woud probably pursue or lye in Wait for Us, I left the Path, and went to the South Westward down the little Miamee River or Creek, where I had fine travelling thro rich Land and beautiful Meadows, in which I coud sometimes see forty or fifty Buffaloes feeding at once—The little Miamee River or Creek continued to run thro the Middle of a fine Meadow, about a Mile wide very clear like an old Field, and not a Bush in it, I coud see the Buffaloes in it above two Miles off: I travelled this Day about 30 M.

Monday 4

This Day I heard several Guns, but was afraid to examine who fired Them, lest they might be some of the French Indians, so I travelled thro the Woods about 30 M ; just at Night I killed a fine barren Cow-Buffaloe and took out her Tongue, and a little of the best of her Meat : The Land still level rich and well timbered with Oak, Walnut, Ash, Locust, and Sugar Trees.

Tuesday 5

I travelled about 30 M.

Wednesday 6

I travelled about 30 M, and killed a fat Bear.

Thursday 7

Set out with my Horse Load of Bear and travelled about 30 M this Afternoon I met a young Man (a Trader) and We encamped together that Night ; He happened to have some Bread with Him, and I had plenty of Meat, so We fared very well.

Friday 8

Travelled about 30 M, and arrived at Night at the Shannoah Town—All the Indians, as well as the white Men came out to welcome my Return to their Town, being very glad that all Things were rightly settled in the Miamee Country, they fired upwards of 150 Guns in the Town, and made an Entertainment in Honour of the late Peace with the western Indians—In my Return from the Twigtwee to the Shannoah Town, I did not keep an exact Account of Course or Distance ; for as the Land thereabouts was every where much the same, and the Situation of the Country was sufficiently described in my Journey to the Twigtwee Town, I thought it unnecessary, but have notwithstanding laid down my Tract pretty nearly in my Plat.

Saturday March 9

In the Shannoah Town, I met with one

of the Mingoe Chiefs, who had been down at the Falls of Ohio, so that We did not see Him as We went up ; I informed Him of the King's Present, and the Invitation down to Virginia—He told that there was a Party of French Indians hunting at the Falls, and if I went there they would certainly kill Me or carry Me away Prisoner to the French; For it is certain they would not let Me pafs : However as I had a great Inclination to see the Falls, and the Land on the E Side the Ohio, I resolved to venture as far as pofsible.

Sunday 10 & Monday 11

Stayed in the Town, and prepared for my Departure.

Tuesday 12

I got my Horses over the River and after Breakfast my Boy and I got ferryed over—The Ohio is near $\frac{1}{4}$ of a Mile wide ot Shannoah Town, & is very deep and smooth.

Wednesday 13

We set out S 45 W, down the said River on the SE Side 8 M, then S 10 M, here I met two Men belonging to Robert Smith at whose House I lodged on this Side the Miamee River, and one Hugh Crawford, the said Robert Smith had given Me an Order upon these Men, for two of the Teeth of a large Beast, which they were bringing from towards the Falls of Ohio, one of which I brought in and delivered to the Ohio Company—Robert Smith informed Me that about seven Years ago these Teeth and Bones of three large Beasts (one of which was somewhat smaller than the other two) were found in a salt Lick or Spring upon a small Creek which runs into the S Side of the Ohio, about 15 M, below the Mouth of the great Miamee River, and 20 above the Falls of Ohio—He afsured Me that the Rib Bones of the largest of these Beasts were eleven Feet long, and the Skull Bone six feet wide, acrofs the Forehead, & the other Bones

in Proportion; and that there were several Teeth there, some of which he called
Horns, and said they were upwards of
five Feet long, and as much as a Man coud
well carry: that he had hid one in a Branch
at some Distance from the Place, lest the
French Indians shoud carry it away—The
Tooth which I brought in for the Ohio
Company, was a Jaw Tooth of better than
four Pounds Weight; it appeared to be
the furthest Tooth in the Jaw, and looked
like fine Ivory when the outside was scraped
off—I also met with four Shannoah Indians
coming up the River in their Canoes, who
informed Me that there were about sixty
French Indians encamped at the Falls.

Thursday 14
I went down the River S 15 M, the Land
upon this Side the Ohio chiefly broken, and
the Bottoms but narrow.

Friday 15
S 5 M. SW 10 M, to a Creek that was
so high, that We coud not get over that
Night.

Saturday 16
S 45 W about 35 M.

Sunday 17
The same Course 15 M, then N 45 W
5 M.

Monday 18
N 45 W 5 M then SW 20 M, to the
lower Salt Lick Creek. which Robert Smith
and the Indians told Us was about 15 M
above the Falls of Ohio; the Land still
hilly, the Salt Lick here much the same
with those before described—this Day We
heard several Guns which made Me ima-
gine the French Indians were not moved,
but were still hunting, and firing thereabouts: We also saw some Traps newly
set, and the Footsteps of some Indians
plain on the Ground as if they had been
there the Day before—I was now much
troubled that I coud not comply with my
Instructions, & was once resolved to leave

the Boy and Horses, and to go privately
on Foot to view the Falls; but the Boy
being a poor Hunter, was afraid he woud
starve if I was long from him, and there was
also great Danger lest the French Indians
shoud come upon our Horses Tracts, or
hear their Bells, and as I had seen good
Land enough, I thought perhaps I might
be blamed for venturing so far, in such
dangerous Times, so I concluded not to
go to the Falls; but travell'd away to the
Southward till We were over the little
Cuttaway River—The Falls of Ohio by the
best Information I coud get are not very
steep, on the SE Side there is a Bar of
Land at some Distance from the Shore, the
Water between the Bar and the Shore is
not above 3 feet deep, and the Stream mo-
derately strong, the Indians frequently paſs
safely in their Canoes thro this Paſsage, but
are obliged to take great Care as they go
down lest the Current which is much the
strongest on the NW Side shoud draw them
that Way; which woud be very dangerous
as the Water on that Side runs with great
Rapidity over several Ledges 'of Rocks;
the Water below the Falls they say is about
six Fathoms deep, and the River continues
without any Obstructions till it empties it-
self into the Miſsisippi which is accounted
upwards of 400 M—The Ohio near the
Mouth is said to be very wide, and the Land
upon both Sides very rich, and in general
very level, all the Way from the Falls—
After I had determined not to go to the
Falls, We turned from Salt Lick Creek, to
a Ridge of Mountains that made towards
the Cuttaway River, & from the Top of the
Mountain We saw a fine level Country SW
as far as our Eyes coud behold, and it was
a very clear Day; We then went down
the Mountain and set out S 20 W about
5 M, thro rich level Land covered with
small Walnut Sugar Trees, Red-Buds, &c.

Tuesday March 19
We set out S and croſsed several Creeks
all running to the SW, at about 12 M,

came to the little Cuttaway River: We were obliged to go up it about 1 M to an Island, which was the shoalest Place We coud find to crofs at, We then continued our Course in all about 30 M thro level rich Land except about 2 M which was broken and indifferent—This Level is about 35 M broad, and as We came up the Side of it along the Branches of the little Cuttaway We found it about 150 M long; and how far toward the SW We coud not tell, but imagined it held as far the great Cuttaway River, which woud be upwards of 100 M more, and appeared much broader that Way than here, as I coud discern from the Tops of the Mountains

Wednesday 20.
We did not travel, I went up to the Top of a Mountain to view the Country, to the SE it looked very broken, and mountainous but to the Eastward and SW it appeared very level.

Thursday 21
Set out S 45 E 15 M, S 5 M, here I found a Place where the Stones shined like high-coloured Brafs, the Heat of the Sun drew out of them a Kind of Borax or Salt Petre only something sweeter; some of which I brought in to the Ohio Company, tho I believe it was Nothing but a Sort of Sulphur.

Friday 22
SE 12 M, I killed a fat Bear, and was taken sick that Night.

Saturday 23
I stayed here, and sweated after the Indian Fashion, which helped Me.

Sunday 24
Set out E 2 M, NE 3 M, N 1 M, E 2 M, SE 5 M, E 2 M, N 2 M, SE 7 M to a small Creek, where We encamped in a Place where We had but poor Food for our Horses, & both We and They were very much wearied: the Reason of our making so many short Courses was,

We were driven by a Branch of the little Cuttaway River (whose Banks were so exceeding steep that it was impofsible to ford it) into a Ledge of rocky Laurel Mountains which were almost impafsable.

Monday 25
Set out SE 12 M, N 2 M, E 1 M, S 4 M, SE 2 M, We killed a Buck Elk here and took out his Tongue to carry with Us.

Tuesday 26
Set out SE 10 M, SW 1 M, SE 1 M, SW 1 M SE 1 M, SW 1 M, SE 1 M SW 1 M SE 5 M killed 2 Buffaloes & took out their Tongues and encamped—These two Days We travelled thro Rocks and Mountains full of Laurel Thickets which We coud hardly creep thro without cutting our Way.

Wednesday 27
Our Horses and Selves were so tired that We were obliged to stay this Day to rest, for We were unable to travel—On all the Branches of the little Cuttaway River was great Plenty of fine Coal some of which I brought in to the Ohio Company.

Thursday 28
Set out SE 15 M crofsing several Creeks of the little Cuttaway River, the Land still full of Coal and black Slate.

Friday 29
The same Course SE about 12 M the Land still mountainous.

Saturday 30
Stayed to rest our Horses, I went on Foot, and found a Pafsage thro the Mountains to another Creek, or a Fork of the same Creek that We were upon.

Sunday 31
The same Course SE 15 M, killed a Buffaloe & encamped.

Monday April 1
Set out the same Course about 20 M,

Part of the Way We went along a Path up the Side of a little Creek, at the Head of which was a Gap in the Mountains, then our Path went down another Creek to a Lick where Blocks of Coal about 8 or 10 In: square lay upon the Surface of the Ground, here We killed a Bear and encamped.

Tuesday 2
Set out S 2 M, SE 1 M, NE 3 M, killed a Buffaloe.

Wednesday 3
S 1 M, SW 3 M, E 3 M, SE 2 M, to a small Creek on which was a large Warriors Camp, that woud contain 70 or 80 Warriors, their Captain's Name or Title was the Crane, as I knew by his Picture or Arms painted on a Tree.

Thursday 4
We stayed here all Day to rest our Horses, and I platted down our Courses and I found I had still near 200 M Home upon a streight Line.

Friday April 5
Rained, and We stayed at the Warrior's Camp.

Saturday 6
We went along the Warrior's Road S 1 M, SE 3 M, S 2 M, SE 3 M, E 3 M, killed a Bear.

Sunday 7
Set out E 2 M, NE 1 M, SE 1 M, S 1 M, W 1 M, SW 1 M, S 1 M, SE 2 M, S 1 M.

Monday 8
S 1 M, SE 1 M, E 3 M. SE 1 M, E 3 M, NE 2 M, N 1 M, E 1 M, N 1 M, E 2 M and encamped upon a small Laurel Creek.

Tuesday 9 & Wednesday 10
The Weather being somewhat bad We did not travel these two Days, the Country being still rocky mountainous, & full of

Laurel Thickets, the worst traveling I ever saw.

Thursday 11
We travelled several Courses near 20 M, but in the Afternoon as I coud see from the Top of the Mountain the Place We came from, I found We had not come upon a streight Line more than N 65 E 10 M.

Friday 12
Set out thro very difficult Ways, E 5 M, to a small Creek.

Saturday 13
The same Course E upon a streight Line, tho the Way We were obliged to travel was near 20 M, here We killed two Bears, the Way still rocky and mountainous.

Sunday 14
As Food was very scarce in these barren Mountains, We were obliged to move for fresh Feeding for our Horses, so We went on E 5 M. then N 20 W 6 M, to a Creek where We got something better Feeding for our Horses, in climbing up the Clifts and Rocks this Day two of our Horses fell down, and were pretty much hurt, and a Paroquete which I had got from the Indians, on the other Side the Ohio (where there are a great many) died of a Bruise he got by a Fall; tho it was but a Trifle I was much concerned at losing Him, as he was perfectly tame, and had been very brisk all the Way, and I had still Corn enough left to feed Him—In the Afternoon I left the Horses, and went a little Way down the Creek, and found such a Precipice and such Laurel Thickets as We coud not pass, and the Horses were not able to go up the Mountain till they had rested a Day or two.

Monday 15
We cut a Passage through the Laurels better than 2 M, as I was climbing up the Rocks, I got a Fall which hurted Me pretty

much—This Afternoon as We wanted Provision I killed a Bear.

Tuesday 16
Thunder and Rain in the Morning—We set out N 25 E 3 M.

Wednesday 17
This Day I went to the Top of a Mountain to view the Way, and found it so bad that I did not care to engage it, but rather chose to go out of the Way and keep down along the Side of a Creek till I coud find a Branch or Run on the other Side to go up.

Thursday 18
Set out down the said Creek Side N 3 M, then the Creek turning NW I was obliged to leave it, and go up a Ridge NE 1 M, E 2 M, SE 2 M, NE 1 M, to the Fork of a River.

Friday 19
Set out down the said Run NE 2 M, E 2 M, SE 2 M, N 20 E 2 M, E 2 M, up a large Run.

Saturday 20
Set out SE 10 M, E 4 M, over a small Creek—We had such bad traveling down this Creek, that We had like to have lost one of our Horses.

Sunday 21
Stayed to rest our Horses.

Monday 22
Rained all Day—We coud not travel.

Tuesday 23
Set out E 8 M along a Ridge of Mountains then SE 5 M, E 3 M, SE 4 M, and encamped among very steep Mountains.

Wednesday 24
SE 4 M thro steep Mountains and Thickets E 6 M.

Thursday 25
E 5 M, SE 1 M, NE 2 M, SE 2 M, E 1 M, then S 2 M, E 1 M killed a Bear.

Friday 26
Set out SE 2 M, here it rained so hard We were obliged to stop.

Saturday 27 Sunday 28 & Monday 29
These three Days it continued raining & bad Weather, so that We coud not travel—All the Way from Salt Lick Creek to this Place, the Branches of the little Cuttaway River were so high that We coud not pass Them, which obliged Us to go over the Heads of them, thro a continued Ledge of almost inaccessable Mountains, Rocks and Laurel Thickets.

Tuesday 30
Fair Weather set out E 3 M, SE 8 M, E 2 M, to a little River or Creek which falls into the big Conhaway, called blue Stone, where we encamped and had good Feeding for our Horses.

Wednesday May 1
Set out N 75 E 10 M and killed a Buffaloe, then went up a very high Mountain, upon the Top of which was a Rock 60 or 70 Feet high, & a Cavity in the Middle, into which I went, and found there was a Passage thro it which gradually ascended to the Top, with several Holes in the Rock, which let in the Light, when I got to the Top of this Rock, I coud see a prodigious Distance, and coud plainly discover where the big Conhaway River broke the next high Mountain, I then came down and continued my Course N 75 E 5 M farther and encamped.

Thursday 2 & Friday 3
These two Days it rained and We stayed at our Camp to take Care of some Provision We had killed.

Saturday 4
This Day our Horses run away, and it

was late before We got Them, so We coud not travel far, We went N 75 E 4 M.

Sunday May 5
Rained all Day.

Monday 6
Set out thro very bad Ways E 3 M, NE 6 M, over a bad Laurel Creek E 4 M.

Tuesday 7
Set out E 10 M, to the big Conhaway or new River and got over half of it to a large Island where We lodged that Night.

Wednesday 8
We made a Raft of Logs and crofsed the other half of the River & went up it S about 2 M—The Conhaway or new River (by some called Wood's River) where I crofsed it (which was about 8 M above the Mouth of blue Stone River) is better than 200 Yards wide, and pretty deep, but full of Rocks and Falls—The Bottoms upon it and blue Stone River are very rich but narrow, the high Land broken.

Thursday 9
Set out E 13 M to a large Indian Warrior's Camp, where We killed a Bear and stayed all Night.

Friday 10
Set out E 4 M. SE 3 M, S 3 M, thro Mountains cover'd with Ivy and Laurel Thickets.

Saturday 11
Set out S 2 M, SE 5 M, to a Creek and a Meadow where We let our Horses feed, then SE 2 M, S 1 M, SE 2 M to a very high Mountain up on the Top of which was a Lake or Pond about $\frac{1}{4}$ of a Mile long NE & SW, & $\frac{1}{4}$ of a Mile wide the Water fresh and clear, and a clean gravelly Shore about 10 Yards wide with a fine Meadow and six fine Springs in it, then S about 4 M, to a Branch of the Conhaway called Sinking Creek.

Sunday 12
Stayed to rest our Horses and dry some Meat We had killed.

Monday 13
Set out SE 2 M, E 1 M, SE 3 M, S 12 M to one Richd Halls in Augusta County this Man is one of the farthest Settlers to the Westward upon the New River.

Tuesday 14
Stayed at Richd Hall's and wrote to the President of Virginia & the Ohio Company to let them know I shoud be with Them by the 15th of June.

Wednesday 15
Set out from Richd Hall's S 16 M.

Thursday 16
The same Course S 22 M and encamped at Beaver Island Creek (a Branch of the Conhaway) opposite to the Head of Roanoke.

Friday 17
Set out SW 3 M, then S 9 M, to the dividing Line between Carolina and Virginia, where I stayed all Night, the Land from Richd Hall's to this Place is broken.

Saturday 18
Set out S 20 M to my own House on the Yadkin River, when I came there I found all my Family gone, for the Indians had killed five People in the Winter near that Place, which frightened my Wife and Family away to Roanoke about 35 M nearer in among the Inhabitants, which I was informed of by an old Man I met near the Place.

Sunday 19
Set out for Roanoke, and as We had now a Path, We got there the same Night where I found all my Family well.

CHRISTOPHER GIST.

Instructions given to Mr Christopher Gist by the Comittee of the Ohio Company

July 16th 1751

AFTER You have returned from Williamsburg and have executed the Comission of the President & Council, if they shall think proper to give You One, otherwise as soon as You can conveniently You are to apply to Colo Cresap for such of the Company's Horses, as You shall want for the Use of yourself and such other Person or Persons You shall think necessary to carry with You; and You are to look out & observe the nearest & most convenient Road You can find from the Company's Store at Wills's Creek to a Landing at Mohongeyela; from thence You are to proceed down the Ohio on the South Side thereof, as low as the Big Conhaway, and up the same as far as You judge proper, and find good Land—You are all the Way to keep an exact Diary & Journal & therein note every Parcel of good Land, with the Quantity as near as You can by any Means compute the same, with the Breadth, Depth, Course and Length of the several Branches falling into the Ohio, & the different Branches any of Them are forked into, laying the same as exactly down in a Plan thereof as You can; observing also the Produce, the several Kinds of Timber and Trees, observing where there is Plenty and where the Timber is scarce; and You are not to omit proper Observations on the mountainous, barren, or broken Land, that We may on your Return judge what Quantity of good Land is contained within the Compass of your Journey, for We woud not have You omit taking Notice of any Quantity of good Land, tho not exceeding 4 or 500 Acres provided the same lies upon the River Ohio & may be convenient for our building Store Houses & other Houses for the better carrying on a Trade and Correspondence down that River.

1751.

PURSUANT to my Instructions hereunto annexed from the Comittee of the Ohio Company bearing Date 16th July 1751

Monday Novr 4

Set out from the Company's Store House in Frederick County Virginia opposite the Mouth of Wills's Creek and crofsing Potomack River went W 4 M to a Gap in the Allegany Mountains upon the SW Fork of the said Creek—This Gap is the nearest to Potomack River of any in the Allegany Mountains, and is accounted one of the best, tho the Mountain is very high, The Ascent is no where very steep but rises gradually near 6 M, it is now very full of old Trees & Stones, but with some Pains might be made a good Waggon Road; this Gap is directly in the Way to Mohongaly, & several Miles nearer than that the Traders comonly pafs thro, and a much better Way.

Tuesday 5

Set out N 80 W 8 M, it rained and obliged Us to stop.

Wednesday 6

The same Course 3 M hard Rain.

Thursday 7

Rained hard and We coud not travel

Friday 8

Set out the same Courses N 80 W 3 M, here We encamped, and turned to see where the Branches lead to & found they descended into the middle Fork of Yaughaughgaine—We hunted all the Ground for

10 M, or more and killed several Deer, & Bears, and one large Elk—The Bottoms upon the Branches are but narrow with some Indian Fields about 2000 Acres of good high Land about a Mile from the largest Branch.

From Saturday 9 to Tuesday 19

We were employed in searching the Lands and discovering the Branches Creeks &c.

Wednesday 20

Set out N 45 W 5 M killed a Deer

Thursday 21

The same Course 5 M the greatest Part of this Day We were cutting our Way thro' a Laurel Thicket and lodged by the Side of one at Night

Friday 22

Set out the same Course N 45 W 2 M and cut our Way thro a great Laurel Thicket to the middle Fork of Yaughyaughgaine then S down the said Fork (crofsing a Run) 1 M, then S 45 W 2 M over the said Fork where We encamped.

Saturday 23

Rested our Horses and examined the Land on Foot, which We found to be tolerable rich & well timbered but stony and broken.

Sunday 24

Set out W 2 M then S 45 W 6 M over the S Fork and encamp'd on the SW Side about 1 M from a small Hunting Town of the Delawares from whom I bought some Corn—I invited these Indians to the Treaty at the Loggs Town, the full Moon in May, as Col^o Patton had desired Me; they treated

Me very civilly, but after I went from that Place my Man informed Me that they threatened to take away our Guns and not let Us travel.

Monday 25
Set out W 6 M, then S 45 W 2 M to a Laurel Creek, where We encamped & killed some Deer.

From Tuesday 26 to Thursday 28
We were examining the Lands which We found to be rocky and mountainous

Friday 29
Set out W 3 M then N 65 W 3 M, N 45 W 2 M.

From Saturday 30 to Friday Decr 6
We searched the Land several Miles round and found it about 15 M from the Foot of the Mountains to the River Mohongaly the first 5 M of which E & W is good level farming Land, with fine Meadows, the Timber white Oak and Hiccory —the same Body of Land holds 10 M, S, to the upper Forks of Mohongaly, and about 10 M, N, towards the Mouth of Yaughyaughgaine—The Land nearer the River for about 8 or 9 M wide, and the same Length is much richer & better timbered, with Walnut, Locust, Poplars and Sugar-Trees, but is in some Places very hilly, the Bottoms upon the River 1 M, and in some Places near 2 M wide.

Saturday 7
Set out W 6 M and went to an Indian Camp and invited them to the Treaty at the Loggs Town at the full Moon in May next ; at this Camp there was a Trader named Charles Poke who spoke the Indian Tongue well, the Indian to whom this Camp belonged after much Discourse with Me, complained & said " my Friend You was " sent to Us last Year from the Great Men " in Virginia to inform Us of a Present " from the Great King over the Water, " and if You can bring News from the

" King to Us, why cant You tell Him " something from Me ? The Proprietor of " Pensylvania granted my Father a Tract " of Land begining eight Miles below " the Forks of Brandy Wine Creek and " binding on the said Creek to the Fork " and including the West Fork & all its " Waters on both Sides to the Head Foun- " tain—The White People now live on " these Lands, and will neither let Me have " Them, nor pay Me any Thing for Them " —My Father's Name was Chickocon- " necon, I am his eldest Son, and my Name " is Nemicotton—I desire that You will " let the Governor and great Men in Vir- " ginia know this—It may be they will tell " the great King of it, and he will make M^r " Pen or his People give Me the Land or " pay Me for it—This Trader here Charles " Poke knows the Truth of what I say, that " the Land was granted to my Father, & " that He or I never sold it, to which " Charles Poke answered that Chickocon- " necon had such a grant of Land, & that " the People who lived on it coud get no " Titles to it, for that it was now called " Mannor Lands—This I was obliged to " insert in my Journal to please the Indian.

Sunday Decr 8
Stayed at the Indian Camp.

Monday 9
Set out S 45 W 1 M, W 6 M to the River Mohongaly—at this Place is a large Cavity in a Rock about 30 Feet long & 20 Feet wide & about 7 Feet high and an even Floor—The Entrance into it is so large and open that it lets in Plenty of Light, and close by it is a Stream of fine Water.

From Tuesday 10 to Friday 13
We were examining the Lands which for 9 or 10 M, E is rich but hilly as before described, on the E Side the River for several Miles there are fine Bottoms a Mile wide and the Hills above them are extraordinary rich and well timbered.

Saturday 14
We had Snow.

Sunday 15
Crossed the River Mohongaly which in this Place is 53 Poles wide, the Bottoms upon the W Side are not above 100 Yards broad, but the Hills are very rich both up and down the River, and full of Sugar Trees.

Monday 16
Spent in searching the Land.

Tuesday 17
Set out W 5 M the Land upon this Course hilly but very rich for about a Mile and a half, then it was level with good Meadows but not very rich for about a Mile & a half more, & the last 2 M next to Licking Creek was very good Land ; upon this Creek We lodged at a hunting Camp of an Indian Captain named Oppaymolleah, here I saw an Indian named Joshua who spoke very good English; he had been acquainted with Me several Years, and seemed very glad to see Me, and wondered much where I was going so far in those Woods ; I said I was going to invite all the great Men of the Indians to a Treaty to be held at Loggs Town, the full Moon in May next, where a Parcel of Goods, a Present from the King of Great Britain, woud be delivered Them by proper Comissioners, and that these were the Goods which I informed them of last Year, by Order of the President of Virginia, Col° Lee, who was since dead. Joshua informed Them what I said, and They told Me, I ought to let the Beaver know this, so I wrote a Line to him by Joshua, who promised to deliver it safe, and said there was a Trader's Man who coud read it for him —This Beaver is the Sachemore or Chief of the Delawares It is customary among the Indian Chiefs to take upon Them the Name of any Beast or Bird they fancy, the Picture of which they always sign instead of their Name or Arms.

55

Wednesday 18
Stayed at the Camp.

Thursday 19
Set out W 3 M, S 45 W 2 M, W 1 M to a Branch of Licking Creek

Friday 20
Set out W 1 M, S 45 W 6 M and encamped.

From Saturday 21 to Tuesday Janʳʸ 7
We stayed at this Place, We had a good Deal of Snow & bad Weather—My Son had the Misfortune to have his Feet frostbitten, which kept Us much longer here than We intended however We kill'd Plenty of Deer Turkeys &c and fared very well—The Land hereabouts very good but to the W & SW it is hilly.

1752
Wednesday Janʳʸ 8
My Son's Feet being somewhat better, We set out S 30 W 5 M, S 45 W 3 M, the Land middling good but hilly—I found my Son's Feet too tender to travel, and We were obliged to stop again.

From Thursday 9 to Sunday 19
We stayed at this Place—While We were here We killed Plenty of Bear Deer & Elk, so that We lived very well.

Monday 20
We set out W 5 M—here We were stopped by Snow.

Tuesday 21
Stayed all the Day in the Camp.

Wednesday 22
Set out S 45 W 12 M, where we scared a Panther from under a Rock where there was Room enough for Us, in it We encamped & had good Shelter.

56

From Thursday 23 to Sunday 26
We stayed at this Place & had Snow & bad Weather.

Monday 27
Set out S 45 W 6 M, here We had Snow & encamped.

From Tuesday 28 to Friday 31
Stayed at this Place, the Land upon these last Courses is rich but hilly and in some Places Stony.

Saturday Febʸ 1
Set out S 45 W 3 M, S 45 E 1 M, S 2 M, S 45 W 1 M, crofsed a Creek on which the Land was very hilly and rocky yet here and there good Spots on the Hills.

Sunday 2
S 45 W 3 M, here We were stopped by Snow

From Monday 3 till Sunday 9
We stayed at this Place and had a good Deal of Snow & bad Weather.

Monday 10
Set out S 45 W 8 M—The Snow hard upon the Top & bad traveling

Tuesday 11
The same Course S 45 W 2 M, then W 1 M, S 45 W 4 M.

Wednesday 12
Killed two Buffaloes and searched the Land to the NW which I found to be rich & well timbered with lofty Walnuts, Ash, Sugar Trees &c but hilly in most Places.

Thursday 13
Set out W 1 M, S 45 W 2 M, W 2 M, S 45 W 2 M, W 2 M—In this Day's Journey We found a Place where a Piece of Land about 100 Yards square & about 10 Feet deep from the Surface had slipped down a steep Hill, somewhat more than it's own Breadth, with most of the Trees standing on it up-

57

right as they were at first, and a good many Rocks which appeared to be in the same Position as they were before the Ground slipt: It had bent down and crushed the Trees as it came along, which might plainly be seen by the Ground on the upper Side of it, over which it had pafsed—It seemed to have been done but two or three Years ago—In the Place from whence it removed was a large Quarry of Rocks, in the Sides of which were Veins of several Colours, particularly one of a deep yellow, about 3 Feet from the Bottom, in which were other small Veins some white, some a greenish Kind of Copperas: A Sample of which I brought in to the Ohio Company in a small Leather Bag Nᵒ 1— Not very far from this Place We found another large Piece of Earth, which had slipped down in the same Manner—Not far from here We encamped in the Fork of a Creek.

Friday 14
We stayed at this Place—On the NW Side of the Creek on a rising Ground by a small Spring We found a large Stone about 3 Feet Square on the Top, and about 6 or 7 Feet high: it was all covered with green Mofs except on the SE Side which was smooth and white as if plaistered with Lime. On this Side I cut with a cold Chizzel in large Letters,

THE OHIO COMPANY
FEBʸ 1751
BY CHRISTOPHER GIST

Saturday 15
Set out S 45 W 5 M, rich Land but hilly, very rich Bottoms up the Creek but not above 200 Yards wide.

Sunday 16
S 45 W 5 M thro rich Land, the Bottoms about ¼ of a Mile wide upon the Creek.

58

Monday 17

The same Course S 45 W 3 M, W 3 M, S 45 W 3 M, S 20 W 3 M, S 8 M, S 45 W 2 M over a Creek upon which was fine Land, the Bottoms about a Mile wide.

Tuesday Feby 18

S 10 M over the Fork of a Creek S 45 W 4 M to the Top of a high Ridge, from whence We coud see over the Conhaway River—Here We encamped, the Land mixed with Pine and not very good.

Wednesday 19

Set out S 15 M, S 45 W 6 M to the Mouth of a little Creek, upon which the Land is very rich, and the Bottoms a Mile wide—The Conhaway being very high overflowed some Part of the Bottoms.

Thursday 20

Set out N 45 W 2 M acrofs a Creek over a Hill, then S 80 W 10 M to a large Run, all fine Land upon this Course—(We were now about 2 M from the River Conhaway) —Then continued our Course S 80 W 10 M, the first 5 M good high Land; tolerably level the last 5 thro the River, Bottoms which were a Mile wide and very rich to a Creek or large Run which We crofsed, & continued our Course S 80 W 2 M farther & encamped.

Friday 21

The same Course S 80 W still continued 8 M further; then S 2 M to the Side of the River Conhaway, then down the said River N 45 W 1 M to a Creek where We encamped—The Bottoms upon the River here are a Mile wide, the Land very rich —The River at this Place is 79 Poles broad.

Saturday 22

Set out N 45 W 4 M, W 7 M, to a high Hill from whence We coud see the River Ohio, then N 45 W 12 M to the River Ohio at the Mouth of a small Run where We encamped. The Bottoms upon the

River here are a Mile wide & very good, but the high Land broken.

Sunday 23

Set out S 45 E 14 M over Letort's Creek—The Land upon this Creek is poor, broken, & full of Pines—Then the same Course S 45 E 10 M and encamped on the River Side upon fine rich Land the Bottoms about a Mile wide.

Monday 24

Set out E 12 M up the River all fine Land the Bottoms about 1½ Miles wide, full of lofty Timber: then N 5 M crofsing Smith's Creek. The Land here is level & good, but the Bottoms upon the River are not above ½ a Mile wide—then N 45 E 8 M to a Creek called Beyansoss where We encamped.

Tuesday 25

We searched the Land upon this Creek which We found very good for 12 or 13 M up it from the River—The Bottoms upon it are about ½ a Mile wide, & the Bottoms upon the River at the Mouth of it a Mile wide, and very well timbered.

Wednesday 26

Set out N 45 E 13 M to the River Ohio at the Mouth of a Creek called Lawwellaconin; then S 55 E 5 M up the said Creek—The Bottoms upon this Creek are a Mile wide & the high Land very good & not much broken, & very well timbered

Thursday 27 Friday 28 & Saturday 29

Rained and We coud not travel—Killed four Buffaloes.

Sunday March 1 and Monday 2

Set out N 30 E 10 M to a little Branch full of Coal then N 30 E 16 M to Nawmissipia or Fishing Creek—My Son hunted up this Creek (where I had cut the Letters upon the Stone) which he said was not above 6 M in a streight Line from this Place—The Bottoms upon this Creek are but narrow, the high Land hilly, but very rich and well timbered.

Tuesday 3

Set out N 30 E 18 M to Molchuconickon or Buffaloe Creek.

Wednesday 4

We hunted up and down this Creek to examine the Land—The Bottoms are ¾ of a Mile wide & very rich, a great many cleared Fields covered with white Clover, the high Land rich but in general hilly.

Thursday 5

Set out N 30 E 9 M to a Creek called Neemokeesy where We killed a black Fox & two Bears—Upon this Creek We found a Cave under a Rock about 150 Feet long & 55 Feet wide; one Side of it open facing the Creek, the Floor dry—We found it had been much used by Buffaloes & Elks who came there to lick a kind of saltish Clay which I found in the Cave, and of which I took a Sample in a Leather Bag N°. 2.

Friday March 6

We stayed at the Cave—Not very far from it We saw a Herd of Elks near 30 one of which my Son killed.

Saturday 7

Set out N 30 E 7 M, to the Ohio River —The Bottoms here were very rich and near 2 M wide; but a little higher up, the Hill seemed very steep, so that We were obliged to leave the River & went E 6 M on very high Land: then N 9 M, thro' very good high Land tolerable level to a Creek called Wealin or Scalp Creek where We encamped.

Sunday 8

We went out to search the Land which We found very good for near 15 M up this Creek from the Mouth of it, the Bottoms above a Mile wide & some Meadows —We found an old Indian Road up this Creek.

Monday 9

Set out N 45 E 18 M to a Creek—The same Course 3 M to another Creek where We encamped—These Creeks the Traders distinguish by the Name of the two Creeks.

Tuesday 10

We hunted up and down these Creeks to examine the Land from the Mouths of Them, to the Place where We had crofsed near the Heads of Them; in our Way to the Conhaway—They run near parallel at about 3 or 4 M, Distance, for upwards of 30 M—The Land between Them all the Way is rich & level, chiefly Low Grounds & finely timbered with Walnuts, Locusts, Cherry Trees, & Sugar Trees

Wednesday 11

Set out E 18 M crofsing three Creeks all good Land but hilly then S 16 M to our old Camp, where my Son had been frost-bitten. After We had got to this Place in our old Tract, I did not keep any exact Account of Course and Distance, as I thought the Rivers & Creeks sufficiently described by my Courses as I came down.

Thursday 12

I set out for Mohongaly crofsed it upon a Raft of Logs from whence I made the best of my Way to Potomack—I did not keep exactly my old Tract but went more to the Eastward & found a much nearer Way Home; and am of Opinion the Company may have a tolerable good Road from Wills's Creek to the upper Fork of Mohongaly, from whence the River is navigable all the Way to the Ohio for large flat-bottomed Boats—The Road will be a little to the Southward of West, and the Distance to the Fork of Mohongaly about 70 M—While I was at Mohongaly in my Return Home an Indian, who spoke good English, came to Me & said—That their great Men the Beaver and Captain Oppamylucah (these are two Chiefs of the Delawares) desired to know where the Indian's

Land lay, for that the French claimed all the Land on one Side the River Ohio & the English on the other Side; and that Oppamylucah asked Me the same Question when I was at his Camp in my Way down, to which I had made him no Answer—I very well remembered that Oppamylucah had asked Me such a Question, and that I was at a Lofs to answer Him as I now also was: But after some Consideration my Friend "said I We are all one King's "People and the different Colour of our "Skins makes no Difference in the King's "Subjects; You are his People as well as "We, if you will take Land & pay the "King's Rights You will have the same "Privileges as the White People have, "and to hunt You have Liberty every "where so that You dont kill the White "Peoples Cattle & Hogs—To this the Indian said, that I must stay at that Place two Days and then He woud come & see Me again, He then went away, and at the two Days End returned as he promised, and looking very pleasant said He woud stay with Me all Night, after He had been with Me some Time He said that the great Men bid Him tell Me I was very safe that I might come and live upon that River where I pleased—That I had answered Them very true for We were all one King's People sure enough & for his Part he woud come to see Me at Wills's Creek in a Month.

March
From Thursday 12 to Saturday 28

We were traveling from Mohongaly to Potomack for as We had a good many Skins to carry & the Weather was bad We traveled but slow

Sunday 29

We arrived at the Company's Factory at Wills's Creek.

CHRISTOPHER GIST

THIS Day came before Me Christopher Gist & made Oath on the holy Evangelists that the two Journals hereunto annexed, both which are signed by the said Christopher Gist; the first containing an Account of his Travels and Discoveries down the River Ohio, & the Branches thereof, for the Ohio Company in the Years 1750 & 1751 together with his Transactions with the Indians and his Return Home. And the other containing an Account of his Travels and Discoveries down the said River Ohio on the SE Side as low as the Big Conhaway made for the s^d Ohio Company in the Years 1751 & 1752 & his return to Wills's Creek on Potomack River (as in a Platt made thereof by the said Christopher Gist and given in to the said Ohio Company may more fully appear) are just & true except as to the Number of Miles, which the said Christopher Gist did not actually measure and therefore cannot be certain of Them, but computed Them in the most exact Manner he coud & according to the best of his Knowledge. Given under my Hand this   Day of   175

www.ingramcontent.com/pod-product-compliance
Lightning Source LLC
Chambersburg PA
CBHW032144080426
42733CB00008B/1197